Nature's Neighborhoods

All About Ecosystems

Welcome to the Seashore

by Ruth Owen

Ruby Tuesday Books

Published in 2016 by Ruby Tuesday Books Ltd.

Editor: Mark J. Sachner
Designer: Emma Randall
Consultant: Judy Wearing, PhD, BEd
Production: John Lingham

Photo credits
FLPA: 8 (bottom), 10–11, 17 (top), 25, 29 (bottom), 30; Istock Photo: 19 (top); Nature Picture Library: 17 (bottom), 22; Public Domain: 20–21, 29 (top), 30; Science Photo Library: 11 (top right); Shutterstock: Cover, 2–3, 4–5, 6–7, 8–9, 12–13, 14–15, 16, 18, 19 (bottom), 21 (right), 23, 24, 26–27, 28, 30, 31.

Library of Congress Control Number: 2015916860

ISBN 978-1-910549-68-1

Printed and published in the United States of America

For further information including rights and permissions requests, please contact our Customer Service Department at 877-337-8577.

Contents

Words shown in **bold** in the text are explained in the glossary.

Welcome to the Seashore

Who and what lives at the seashore?

This **habitat** is home to many different types of seaweed.

The residents of this habitat include seabirds, crabs, and sea stars, which are also called starfish.

Every living thing at the seashore gets what it needs to live from its habitat.

The seashore is a type of ecosystem. An ecosystem includes all the living things in an area. It also includes non-living things such as water, rocks, and sunlight. Everything in an ecosystem has its own part to play.

So let's find out what happens in this natural neighborhood ...
... welcome to the seashore!

The Tide Goes Out

At the seashore, waves are crashing against the rocky cliffs.

Then, the **tide** slowly starts to go out, uncovering a beach and craggy rocks.

Rocks

Tide pool

Some seawater gets left behind and forms tide pools between the rocks.

When the tide goes out, seals sunbathe and rest on the rocks.

Seagulls swoop down from the cliffs to search for food on the rocks.

Seal

Seagull

At the seashore, the ocean comes in and goes out two times every day. It takes about 12 hours for the water to come close to the shore and then go back out again.

What do you think could be living in a tide pool?

7

Too Tiny to See!

When you peer into a tide pool, you might spot some seaweed or a crab.

Many of the living things, however, are too tiny to see with your eyes alone.

These **microscopic** tide pool residents are **plankton**.

This photo of plankton was taken with a microscope.

Some of the plankton are plant-like living things called **algae**.

They float in water and use sunlight to make their own food inside themselves.

A pint (0.5 liter) of tide pool water can be home to one million microscopic algae!

Tide pool

Tide pools are also home to zooplankton. What do you think this could be?

Microscopic Ocean Animals

A tide pool is home to millions of tiny, floating animals called zooplankton.

Most zooplankton can only be seen with a microscope.

Some of these animals, such as copepods, stay tiny for their whole lives.

A copepod

Zooplankton feed on microscopic algae and on each other. Some zooplankton feed on tiny bits of dead ocean animals.

This photo was taken with a microscope.

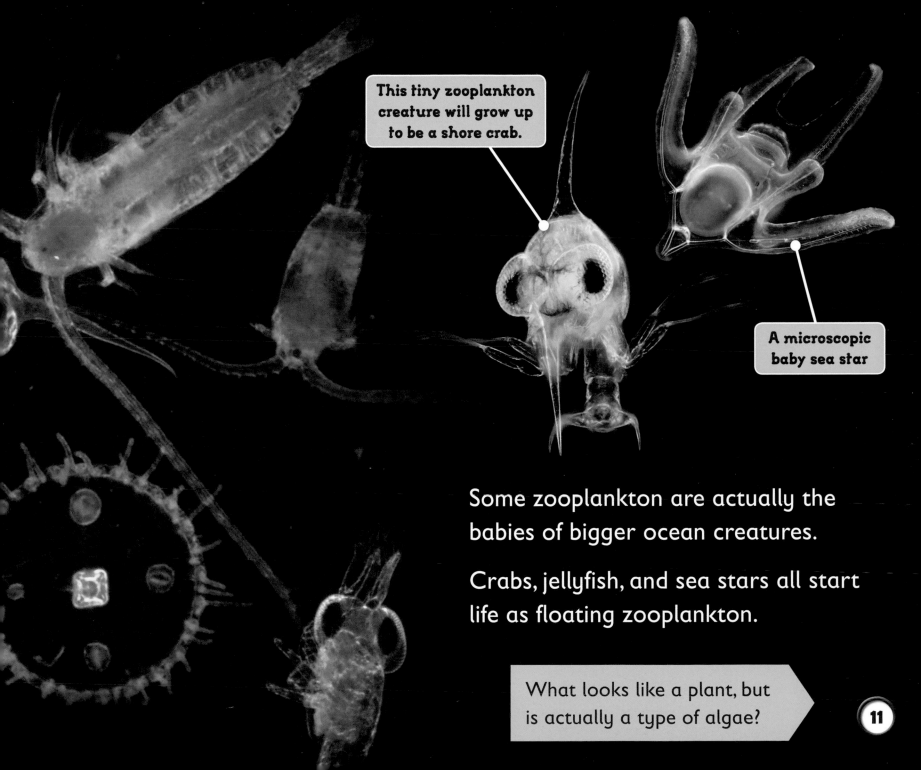

This tiny zooplankton creature will grow up to be a shore crab.

A microscopic baby sea star

Some zooplankton are actually the babies of bigger ocean creatures.

Crabs, jellyfish, and sea stars all start life as floating zooplankton.

What looks like a plant, but is actually a type of algae?

11

All About Seaweed

A tide pool is home to green, red, and brown seaweeds.

Most types of seaweed look like plants, but they are actually algae.

Seaweeds cling to rocks or the sandy seabed with a part called a holdfast.

Seaweed

Seaweeds make the food they need for energy inside themselves. To do this, they use sunlight. Some fish, crabs, seabirds, and other seashore animals eat seaweed.

When the tide goes out, seaweed becomes a hiding place for crabs and other tide pool animals.

They hide under seaweed from seabirds that try to eat them.

What else do you think is clinging to the rocks in a tide pool?

13

Clinging to the Rocks

The rocks around a tide pool may have thousands of mussels and limpets clinging to them.

Mussels are soft-bodied animals with blackish-blue shells.

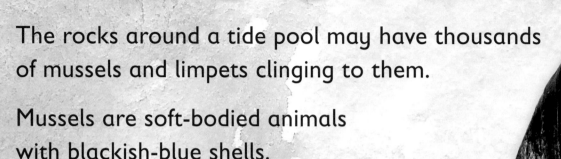

Soft body parts inside shell

A mussel

Two-part shell

When the tide comes in, mussels feed on plankton in the ocean water.

Each limpet has its own spot on a rock that is its home.

It holds onto the rock so tight that it is difficult for birds and other **predators** to remove it!

A limpet's soft body

Shell

A limpet clinging to a rock

Once the tide comes in, a limpet moves around underwater feeding on seaweed. Before the tide goes out again, it returns home. It finds the exact spot on the rocks where it usually lives.

A barnacle is an animal that clings to rocks and doesn't move around. How does it catch its food?

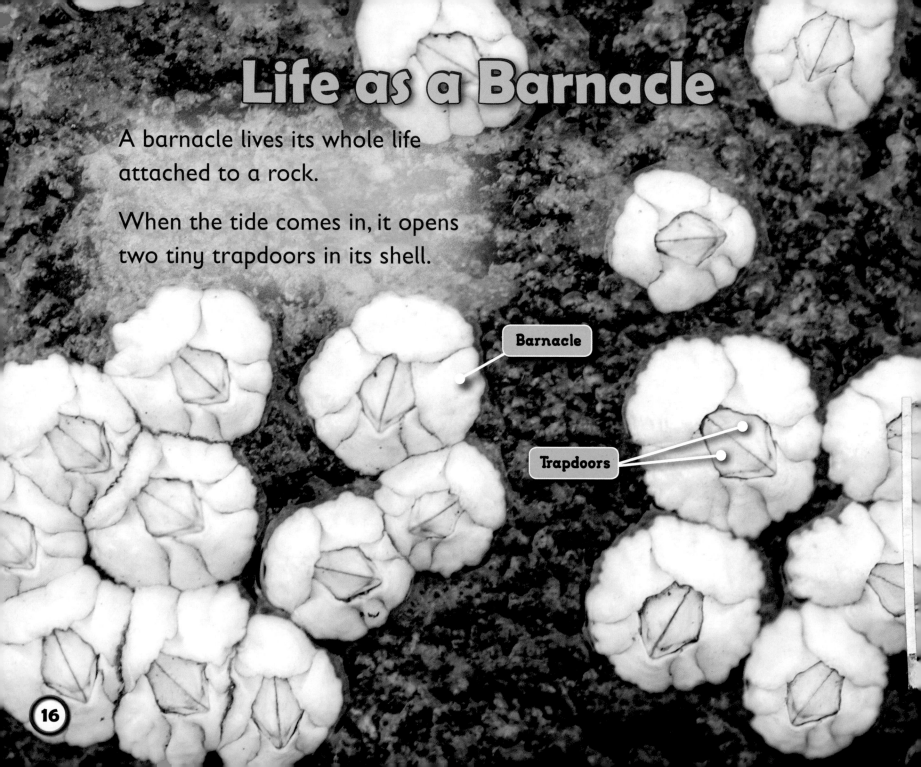

Life as a Barnacle

A barnacle lives its whole life attached to a rock.

When the tide comes in, it opens two tiny trapdoors in its shell.

Barnacle

Trapdoors

The barnacle's 12 legs emerge from the shell.

Then it grabs plankton from the ocean water with its legs.

When the tide goes back out, the barnacle shuts its trapdoors to stay safe from predators.

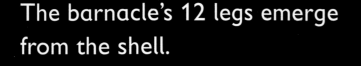

Microscopic baby barnacles

Legs

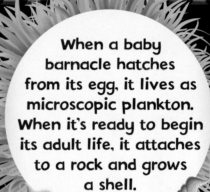

When a baby barnacle hatches from its egg, it lives as microscopic plankton. When it's ready to begin its adult life, it attaches to a rock and grows a shell.

What animals look like flowers and stars and munch on their tide pool neighbors?

Hungry Hunters

Sea anemones and sea stars are hunters that live in tide pools.

Sea anemone

Mouth

Stinging tentacles

A sea anemone is an animal that uses arm-like tentacles to grab small fish and other **prey**. The tentacles sting the prey to **paralyze** it. Then the anemone eats the stunned creature.

A sea star has caught a mussel.

Using the tiny feet on its underside, it pulls open the mussel's shell.

Then the sea star pushes its own stomach out through its mouth and into the shell.

Juices from the sea star's stomach turn the mussel into a soupy mush.

Then the sea star sucks its stomach and its mushy meal back into its mouth.

Mussel

A sea star's mouth is on its underside.

Tiny feet

Some of these barnacle shells have a hole in the top and are empty. What has happened here?

19

A Dog Whelk Goes Hunting

A dog whelk is a predatory water snail that feeds on barnacles, limpets, and mussels.

The whelk has a hard, rough body part called a radula.

It uses its radula to bore a hole in its prey's shell.

The whelk also produces a chemical that can dissolve the shell.

Once the whelk has broken through the shell, it feeds on its prey's soft body.

Dog whelks

Empty barnacle shells

A dog whelk isn't only a tide pool predator, it's also prey. Crabs and seabirds, such as oystercatchers, feed on dog whelks, mussels, barnacles, and limpets.

An oystercatcher

When is a dog whelk not a dog whelk?

21

When Is a Dog Whelk Not a Dog Whelk?

When it's a hermit crab living in a dog whelk shell.

Dog whelk shell

A hermit crab

A hermit crab has a soft body, but no shell to protect it from predators.

The crab searches its habitat for empty shells that once belonged to its neighbors.

When it finds one that's a perfect fit, it moves in!

As a hermit crab grows, it gets too large for its borrowed shell. So it finds a new, bigger shell and moves in. Its old shell may be useful to a younger, smaller hermit crab.

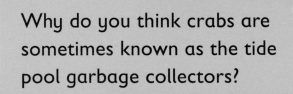

Why do you think crabs are sometimes known as the tide pool garbage collectors?

A Tide Pool Clean-Up Crew

Many types of crabs eat almost anything!

Shore crabs feed on dog whelks, barnacles, and other tide pool neighbors.

If a dead fish or other animal washes into the pool, shore crabs eat this, too.

That's why they get the nickname of garbage collectors.

The hungry shore crabs help keep a tide pool clean.

Shore crab

A female shore crab

A female shore crab lays about 200,000 eggs. She carries the eggs under her body. When the baby crabs hatch, they live as zooplankton until they grow bigger.

Eggs

What other seashore residents help keep the neighborhood clean?

25

Gulls Drop in for Dinner

The seashore is home to herring gulls, or seagulls.

These large birds eat fish, crabs, sea stars—anything that lives in a tide pool!

They also feed on dead animals and human garbage.

A seagull eating a dead fish

Seagulls often fight over food and steal scraps from each other.

A seagull eating a sea star

Mother seagull

Chick

Seagulls build nests of grass and seaweed on rocky cliffs and the roofs of seashore buildings. The parent birds spit up mushy food for their chicks to eat.

What do you think a seagull does when the tide comes in?

The Tide Comes In

When the tide starts to come back in, waves wash in and out over the tide pools.

Finally, the tide pools disappear underwater.

The residents of the seashore are changing all the time. As new animals get washed in by the tide, others get washed out.

Seagulls bob up and down on the ocean searching for floating snacks.

Under the surface, the tide pool seaweed floats in the water.

A fish called a monkeyface eel feeds on the seaweed.

Monkeyface eel

For now, the tide pools are part of the ocean.

But soon the tide will turn again ....

A Seashore Food Web

A food web shows who eats who in an ecosystem.

This food web diagram shows the connections between some of the living things at the seashore.

The arrows mean: **eaten by**

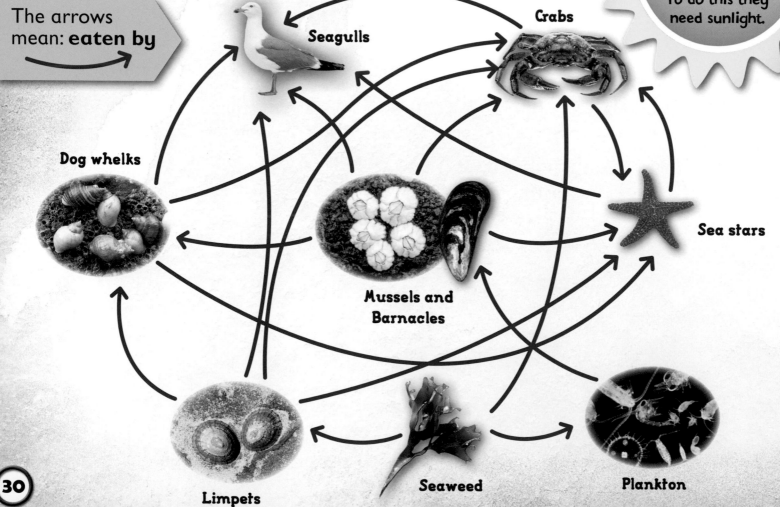

Seagulls

Crabs

Dog whelks

Mussels and Barnacles

Sea stars

Limpets

Seaweed

Plankton

Glossary

algae (AL-gee) Plant-like living things that mostly grow and live in water. Like plants, algae can make their own food using sunlight. Seaweed is a type of algae.

habitat (HAB-uh-tat) The place where living things, such as animals and plants, live and grow. A seashore, pond, or forest is a type of habitat.

microscopic (mye-kruh-SKOP-ik) Able to be seen only with a microscope, not with the eyes alone.

paralyze (PA-ruh-lize) To make an animal or person unable to move.

plankton (PLANGK-tuhn) Microscopic living things, such as animals and algae, that float in water.

predator (PRED-uh-tur) An animal that hunts and eats other animals.

prey (PREY) An animal that is hunted by other animals for food.

tide (TIDE) The rise or fall of the ocean that causes the water to come closer to the shore or move farther away. The tide comes in and goes out twice in every 24 hours.

Index

Read More

Lunis, Natalie. *Crawling Crabs (No Backbone! The World of Invertebrates).* New York: Bearport Publishing (2008).

Spilsbury, Louise. *Tide Pool (Look Inside).* North Mankato, MN: Heinemann-Raintree (2013).

Learn More Online

To learn more about life at the seashore, go to
www.rubytuesdaybooks.com/habitats